To Mom,

Happy Mothers Day

2000!

LITTLE WONDERS

THE WONDER OF

Mom

Phyllis Hobe

The C.R. Gibson Company
Norwalk, Connecticut 06856

LITTLE WONDERS

The Wonder of Mom
The Wonder of Dad
The Wonder of Friends
The Wonder of Babies
The Wonder of Little Girls
The Wonder of Little Boys

Published by The C.R. Gibson Company,
Norwalk, Connecticut 06856

Printed in the U.S.A.
Designed by Deborah Michel

ISBN 0-8378-7701-6
GB401

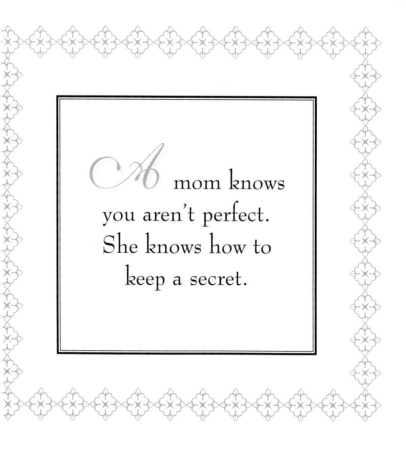

A mom knows
you aren't perfect.
She knows how to
keep a secret.

A mom never runs
out of chocolate chip
cookies, but sometimes
it's hard to find where
she put them.

A mom is never afraid of
thunder and lightning—
when you are.

❧

A mom will warm your hands
in hers before she asks what
happened to your mittens.

A mom can enjoy reading your favorite book out loud for the hundredth time.

A mom may
not always be able
to solve your problems,
but she'll tell you
bedtime stories
that do.

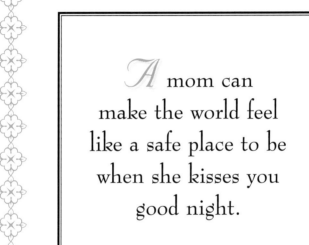

A mom can
make the world feel
like a safe place to be
when she kisses you
good night.

A mom really believes that vegetables are delicious.

❧

A mom knows that nobody ever gets tired of peanut butter and jelly sandwiches.

Nobody can be
in two places at once,
but a mom manages to
be at every game—
yours, your brother's
and your sister's.

A mom cheers
too loud and you wish
she didn't but you're
glad she did.

A mom wants you to pick the kind of dog she likes because she's going to end up taking care of it.

A mom puts an
ad in the newspaper
for the stray kitten you
found, but she's happy
for you when nobody
answers it.

A MOM IS A LIVING HISTORY BOOK—SHE KNOWS NAMES, AGES, WIVES, HUSBANDS, CHILDREN, RECIPES, GOLF SCORES, BASEBALL TEAMS, AND THE BAD GRUDGES, FONDEST MEMORIES AND PET PEEVES

OF EVERY AUNT, UNCLE,
NIECE, NEPHEW AND COUSIN
ON HER SIDE OF THE FAMILY
AND YOUR FATHER'S—AND
SHE'LL TELL YOU WHAT YOU
NEED TO KNOW, WHEN YOU
NEED TO KNOW IT TO GET
ALONG WITH ALL OF THEM.

A mom is better than chicken soup when you're sick.

A mom knows how to say "No" without ever using the word.

A mom's pocketbook is a first aid kit, a file cabinet, a lost-and-found department, a beauty salon and a treasure chest.

A MOM CAN DRIVE YOU TO SCHOOL, DROP CLOTHES OFF AT THE CLEANERS, FILL UP THE GAS TANK, RETURN YOUR BOOK TO THE LIBRARY, PICK UP THE NOTEBOOK YOU LEFT IN THE DENTIST'S OFFICE, AND STILL GET TO WORK ON TIME.

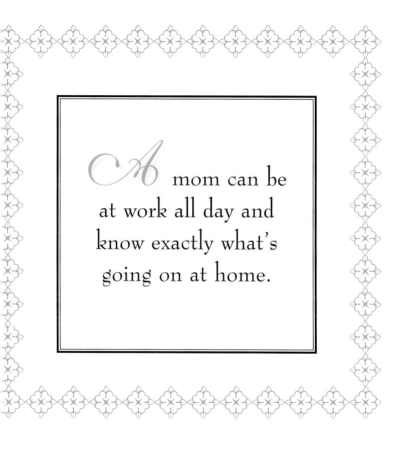

A mom can be at work all day and know exactly what's going on at home.

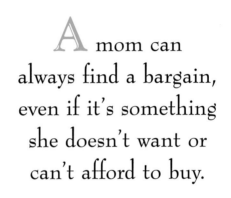

A mom can always find a bargain, even if it's something she doesn't want or can't afford to buy.

A mom says "I love you" in ways like: "Get out of those wet clothes..." "Put a coat on..." "Did you finish your homework?..." "Wash your hands before you eat..." "Let me take your temperature..." "Where are you going?"

A mom leaves
the hall light on when
you decide you're big
enough to go to bed
in the dark.

A mom doesn't like:
what all your friends
are wearing, untied
shoelaces,excuses, bad
manners and unkindness
to other kids.

A MOM LIKES:
WHAT YOU WORE LAST
YEAR AND STILL FITS, CLEAN
SNEAKERS, MADE BEDS,
KIDS WHO SAY, "THANK
YOU" AND KINDNESS
TO OTHER KIDS.

A mom will listen to your excuses, and when you're all finished, she'll still tell you to do what you were supposed to do in the first place.

A mom is always open to another point of view—but it won't change her mind.

A mom is
there to welcome
each and every new
tooth and to be surprised
at what the Tooth
Fairy left for you.

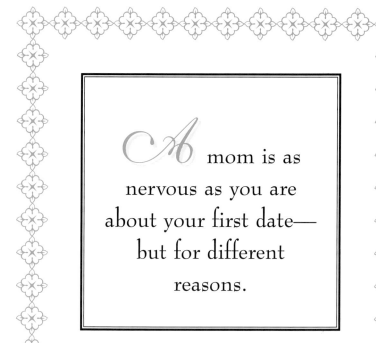

A mom is as nervous as you are about your first date— but for different reasons.

A mom isn't afraid to sit in the passenger seat after you get your driver's license and even if she is, she'll sit there anyway.

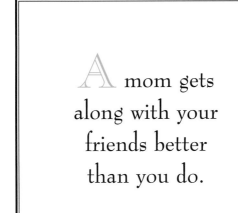

A mom gets
along with your
friends better
than you do.

A mom answers your letters—every time—and writes even if you don't.

❧

A mom lets you call collect—but not every night.

A mom knows where she put those awful baby pictures of you but forgets where she put those recent snapshots of her.

A mom knows that one of these days she has to let you go, which is just about the time you start holding on—that's when a mom becomes a friend.

A mom is like a safety net when you aim too high—she won't let you get hurt no matter how far you fall.

A mom knows how to deal with limitations—she ignores them.

A mom doesn't come right out and say you made a mistake... she'll wait for you to find that out for yourself—unless you take too long.

A mom can
turn a bad day
into a memory just
by listening to you
talk about it.

A mom will order the cheapest thing on the menu when you're buying.

A mom can't be
bothered with maps, and
she pays no attention to street
names and route numbers—
but she always gets to where
she wants to go.

A mom remembers every-
thing you like even if you can't
remember telling her.

❦

A mom is always there, but
tries not to be in your way.

A mom can make unexpected guests feel as if they've been invited to a feast.

A mom can think of a hundred reasons why you ought to pick a college that's closer to home, and can think of a million ways to tell her friends how smart you are for being accepted, but she can't think of a single reason why you can't come home more often.

A mom keeps asking you "what's the matter" as long as you keep insisting that nothing is.

$\mathcal{A}$ mom can
handle criticism,
as long as it isn't
about you.

A mom is never
surprised when you
do something special
because she always knew
you could and would.

A mom gets hurt
whenever you do.

☙

A mom can hide her
fears behind a smile.

A mom will
help you fix your
hurts before she
realizes she has some
of her own.

A mom gets better with
age—yours and hers.

A mom doesn't
have to be in style—
she has a style of her own.

A mom lets
your kids break all the
rules she made when
you were a kid.

A mom may
worry when you go
on a diet, but she's the
first one to comment
on how good
you look.

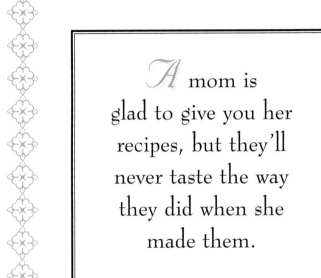

A mom is glad to give you her recipes, but they'll never taste the way they did when she made them.

A mom keeps pictures
of everyone but herself.

———

A mom can turn any kind
of space into a family room
just by being there.

A mom will come and stay with the kids when you need a break—even if it means giving up the break she was going to give herself.

A mom doesn't expect you to thank her, but it's the nicest surprise you can give her.

A mom listens
with her eyes, a mom
listens with her heart—
that's how she hears
what you can't put
into words.